# IRISH C~~

*A History fro~*

Copyright © 2020 by Hourly History.

All rights reserved.

# Table of Contents

Introduction
Background
World War I and the Easter Rising
The War of Independence and the Anglo-Irish Treaty
The Attack on the Four Courts
Civil War Breaks Out
A Bloody Guerilla War
The Deaths of Arthur Griffith and Michael Collins
Executions and Assassinations
The End of the Civil War
Aftermath
Conclusion

# Introduction

All civil wars are, by their very nature, divisive and often fought with great brutality and hatred. That was certainly true of the civil war which took place in Ireland between June 1922 and May 1923. During this bloody internecine conflict, murder, assassination and arbitrary execution became almost commonplace as two groups of Irish people who had fought together in the War of Independence fought against each other to establish the nature and identity of the modern state of Éire.

The divisions which led to the civil war continued to influence Irish politics for much of the twentieth century and led indirectly to the violence which afflicted Northern Ireland during the same period. The Irish Civil War was never formally ended by a treaty or by the surrender of either side, and it left behind a legacy of bitterness and distrust. So deep were the wounds caused by the civil war that, although it was an important part of the struggle for Irish independence, this conflict is rarely spoken about or commemorated in Ireland, and until the 2000s, it was relatively rarely studied by Irish historians.

Until the civil war, the Catholic people of Ireland had been largely united in a fight against British rule. In the civil war, for the first time, they fought one another. This war was fought between former colleagues and frequently between different members of the same extended families. Therein lies the cause of much of the bitterness and resentment, but this also makes the Irish Civil War difficult for outsiders to understand. To make sense of what happened in those 11 months in the early 1920s, it is also necessary to put these events in the context of what had come before and what came after.

This is a confused and confusing story, but it is also crucial to understanding the background of the creation of an independent Ireland. This is the story of the Irish Civil War.

# Chapter One

# Background

*"No person knows better than you do that the domination of England is the sole and blighting curse of this country."*

—Daniel O'Connell

The island of Ireland lies just 50 miles from mainland Britain, across the Irish Sea, but the history of these two islands is very different. Ireland has its own heritage, culture, language, and religion, but for much of its recent history, it was an often-unwilling part of the British Empire.

The association between Ireland and England first began in 1172 when the pope appointed King Henry II of England the feudal lord of Ireland. This gave the English king the right to own land in Ireland and to impose English laws on the people of that country. It wasn't until 1542 that Henry VIII became the first English king to be inaugurated as the king of Ireland, but the reign of Henry VIII also saw England become separated from the Catholic Church of Rome as part of the English Reformation.

By the time that Henry VIII's daughter Elizabeth became queen of England in 1558, England had become a Protestant country with the monarch as the head of the Church of England. The reformation did not spread to Ireland which remained mainly Catholic. This led to a situation where a Gaelic-speaking, largely Catholic majority were ruled by English-speaking Protestant incomers from England who also became the main landowners.

During the English Revolution of 1688, there were a number of battles between Catholics who supported King James II and Protestants who fought for William of Orange. Those who supported James II were finally defeated at the Battle of the Boyne, but the revolution led to many British politicians regarding Ireland as a potential source of rebellion. Draconian laws were enacted which meant that Catholics in Ireland were unable to vote or to join the British Army.

The success of the American colonists in the War of Independence in 1776 and the outbreak of the French Revolution in the late 1700s encouraged a rebellion in Ireland against British rule in 1798. This rebellion was successfully repressed during a bloody conflict which saw many arbitrary executions and massacres of civilians. As many as 30,000 people are thought to have died before the rebellion was finally suppressed. This led directly to the Act of Union in 1800 which removed the remaining vestiges of Irish independence and subsumed Ireland as a part of the United Kingdom, without a parliament of its own.

In the period 1845-1849, Ireland suffered a terrible famine caused by successive failures of the potato crop. Up to a quarter of the population emigrated or died as a direct result of starvation or disease. Most of those affected were poor Catholic families in the south and west, and this famine left a legacy of resentment against the British government which continued to export huge quantities of food from Ireland, failing to provide sufficient food to feed those affected by the famine.

The famine polarized differences in Ireland, between poor, Gaelic-speaking Catholics and more affluent English-speaking Protestant landowners across the country as well as between Ulster, the six counties in the north of Ireland which had a largely Protestant population, and the south and west which was mainly Catholic.

Emigrants from Ireland who had gone to America formed the Fenian Brotherhood which supplied arms that were used in an abortive rebellion against British rule in 1867. The failure of this rebellion led to the emergence of the Irish Home Rule Movement around 1870. This movement supported not a complete break with Britain, but instead the establishment of some form of self-government for Ireland while remaining within the United Kingdom. During the latter part of the nineteenth century, this movement pursued home rule through the British Parliament, and under the Liberal government of William Ewart Gladstone, it came close to achieving this.

However, the issue of independence for Ireland was complicated by the fact that the Protestant majority in the six counties of Ulster was vehemently opposed to separation from the United Kingdom and did not want to be part of a united, independent Ireland ruled from Dublin. By the beginning of the twentieth century, the situation in Ireland remained in a stalemate. The Catholic majority in the south and west wanted some form of self-rule. The Protestant majority in the increasingly industrialized counties of Ulster were committed to maintaining the union between Ireland and the United Kingdom. Both sides began to form groups of armed fighters to protect their interests.

## Chapter Two
# World War I and the Easter Rising

> *"We are out for Ireland for the Irish. But who are the Irish? Not the rack-renting, slum-owning landlord; not the sweating, profit-grinding capitalist; not the sleek and oily lawyer; not the prostitute pressman – the hired liars of the enemy. Not these are the Irish upon whom the future depends. Not these, but the Irish working class, the only secure foundation upon which a free nation can be reared."*
>
> —James Connolly

During the early years of the twentieth century, the issue of home rule for Ireland was the subject of intense debate and political maneuvering within the British Parliament. In Ireland, there was sporadic though mainly small-scale violence as armed supporters of self-rule in the south clashed with Unionists in the north.

In Ulster, the Ulster Volunteers were formed—armed militia groups who vowed to resist, by force if necessary, any attempt by the British government to impose self-rule on the six counties. In 1913, these militias were consolidated into the Ulster Volunteer Force (UVF) and received a clandestine shipment of 25,000 rifles.

In the south and partly in response to the formation of the UVF, a militia group of Nationalists was formed, the Irish Volunteer Force (IVF). This group was also well-armed, and several shipments of rifles and ammunition which originated in Germany were brought to Ireland for their use—Erskine Childers, author of the popular thriller *The Riddle of the Sands* and an ardent Irish Nationalist, personally brought a shipment of 1,000 German rifles to Dublin. By mid-1914, the Irish Volunteer Force had almost 200,000 members.

The potential for an armed confrontation between these two groups was very apparent when, in August 1914, World War I began. Many men of the UVF joined the British Army. The IVF was split between those who believed that they should support the British war effort and those who believed that while Britain was occupied with its war against Germany and Austria-Hungary, Ireland should pursue the fight for independence. Many men of the IVF joined the British Army and fought in the Irish Division in Flanders, often fighting side by side with their former enemies in the UVF. However, a smaller group of Nationalists who were supported by the Irish Republican Brotherhood (IRB) called for neutrality and refused to fight for Britain.

In April of 1916, the Irish Republican Brotherhood, supported by armed members of the Irish Volunteers, seized several public buildings in Dublin and proclaimed an Irish Republic. For six days, there was intense fighting in Dublin as the British Army used heavy weapons to crush the rebellion. Almost 500 people died in the fighting during

Easter Week, many of them civilians, and parts of Dublin were left in ruins by shellfire and subsequent fires.

The Easter Rising was quickly suppressed, and the British arrested over 3,000 people as a result. The majority of these were interned without trial at camps in England and Wales, and between May 3 and 12, 16 of the leaders of the insurrection were executed by firing squad. In August 1916, Sir Roger Casement, a former British diplomat and an early advocate for human rights, was executed for treason for his part in supporting the rebellion.

The executions of Casement and the other leaders of the Easter Rising inflamed opinion in Ireland against the British, and this was reinforced when accounts began to emerge of atrocities carried out by British soldiers. During the night of April 28, British soldiers of the South Staffordshire Regiment entered houses on North King Street in Dublin and shot or bayoneted to death 15 unarmed men. No British soldiers were ever held to account for this massacre. On April 25, a captain in the British Army, John Bowen-Colthurst, arbitrarily shot several unarmed men including two journalists and a city councilor and later ordered the summary execution of the popular Irish writer Francis Sheehy-Skeffington. He was later court-martialed and found to be guilty of murder. Bowen-Colthurst was sentenced to serve 20 months in a secure mental institution.

The Easter Rising was followed by a virtual British occupation of parts of Dublin which further increased the resentment of the people who lived there. Many had not supported the Irish Volunteers and most were completely taken by surprise at the rebellion, but the heavy-handed

British response helped to push public opinion toward support for opposition to British rule.

One of the groups which benefitted from this resentment was Sinn Féin, an Irish political movement which sought to bring together all Irish Nationalists. The group had put forward a candidate in at least one by-election before the war, but by 1916, it had gained little support. However, although Sinn Féin had no involvement in or knowledge of the Easter Rising, it was blamed for this in the British press. Ironically, this had the effect of increasing support for Sinn Féin in Ireland. When in March of 1918, the British government ordered the arrest of leading members of the organization, accusing them of involvement in a plot to support Germany (this was completely untrue), support for Sinn Féin in Ireland increased even further.

When a general election was held in December 1918, Sinn Féin candidates won 73 of the 105 seats representing Ireland in the British Parliament. All the Sinn Féin members of parliament refused to take their seats at Westminster and instead, in January 1919, the Sinn Féin MPs gathered at the Mansion House in Dublin and announced that they were forming the Dáil Éireann, the parliament of Ireland. They announced that Ireland was a republic and appointed a *príomh aire* (prime minister). This action was not recognized by the British government.

In local council elections in 1920, Sinn Féin took control of councils of ten of Ireland's twelve cities. Only Belfast and Derry, both in Ulster, remained in the control of Unionists. It was clear that, whatever the British government may have wanted, Ireland was moving toward self-rule and perhaps full independence.

# Chapter Three

# The War of Independence and the Anglo-Irish Treaty

*"To me the task is a loathsome one. I go, I go in the spirit of a soldier who acts against his best judgement at the orders of his superior."*

—Michael Collins, on being told that he was to attend treaty negotiations

The Irish Volunteers, the group which fought in the failed Easter Rising, was re-formed in 1917 as the Irish Republican Army (IRA) and claimed to have 70,000 members. Raids by IRA members to steal guns and ammunition brought them into frequent conflict with the Royal Irish Constabulary (RIC), the armed police force responsible for keeping order across Ireland, as well as British troops stationed there.

As the First World War drew to a close, Britain considered bringing in conscription in Ireland in order to replace the huge losses suffered in the German Spring Offensive of 1918. This caused outrage in Ireland where, for many people, the British Army was seen as the enemy. During protests and riots against conscription, six civilians were killed and more than one thousand were arrested. On Armistice Day in 1918, which marked the end of the war, while there were celebrations in most British cities, in Dublin there was rioting which left more than one hundred British soldiers injured.

When the first Dáil Éireann met in January 1919, in addition to claiming that Ireland was now a republic, the Sinn Féin MPs also noted in a statement that there was an "existing state of war, between Ireland and England." Almost at the same time, a group of armed IRA men attacked two RIC officers in County Tipperary who were escorting a consignment of explosives. The two RIC men were shot dead. The British government responded by announcing that South Tipperary was a Special Military Area and subject to military rule and law.

This act is now considered the beginning of what has become known as the Irish War of Independence—a guerilla war fought between the members of the IRA and the RIC and British troops. During 1919, there were some instances of violent confrontation, mainly aimed at the RIC. Eleven RIC men were killed and many more wounded. Even more effective was a policy of ostracism against members of the RIC announced by the Dáil in April 1919. The mainly Catholic members of the force found themselves and their families excluded from the communities in which they lived, and the situation became so serious that some were only able to buy food at gunpoint. Resignations from the RIC increased and new members became very difficult to find.

By early 1920, armed attacks by the IRA on RIC barracks, especially small isolated barracks in rural areas, had become so aggressive that most were abandoned, leaving the IRA in effective control of much of south and west Ireland. The British government responded by sending auxiliary paramilitary units to Ireland, including the RIC Special Reserve. This was a unit formed mainly of British World War I veterans who were sent to Ireland to support the RIC. The combination of the dark uniforms of the RIC and the khaki of the Special Reserve led to these units being known as the "Black and Tans," and they rapidly became one of the most feared and hated organizations in Ireland.

From their formation in March 1920, the Black and Tans quickly gained a reputation for drunkenness, ill-discipline, and extreme violence, often directed at the civilian population. Because it was often difficult to engage the IRA due to their hit-and-run tactics, the Black and Tans instead attacked towns thought to be supporting the rebels. During the summer of 1920, several small towns including Balbriggan and Trim were attacked and burned. When in November 1920 an IRA unit under the command of the charismatic leader Michael Collins mounted an attack in Dublin that resulted in the death of 19 people including police officers and British soldiers, the RIC responded by driving into the football ground in Dublin while a match was in progress and shooting indiscriminately into the crowd, killing 14 and injuring more than 60. At the same time, three Nationalist prisoners being held in Dublin Castle were "shot while trying to escape."

In the six months that followed what became known as "Bloody Sunday," violence in Ireland reached a peak. Attacks by the IRA on the RIC continued, as did arrests, internments, and killings of IRA members by the RIC and units of the British Army. However, by May 1921, it had become clear that while the IRA were not strong enough to seize control of Ireland by main force, neither could the British Army defeat an organization which had widespread support amongst the people of Ireland—in a general election for the parliament of Southern Ireland on May 13, Sinn Féin took 124 seats out of 128.

By this point, the IRA was running short of weapons and ammunition while the British were weary of constant casualties and the high cost of maintaining a military presence in Ireland. On July 11, 1921, a truce was agreed and fighting finally ended in Ireland. The truce was followed by extended discussions between the British government and representatives from Ireland. Éamon de Valera, the man appointed as president of the Republic of Ireland by the Dáil, sent a delegation headed by two men to negotiate—Michael Collins, who had become one of the leading members of the IRA, and Arthur Griffith, one of the founders of Sinn Féin.

Negotiations lasted several months and produced the Anglo-Irish Treaty. Under this treaty, Ireland was to become the Irish Free State with its own House of Commons, but it would still be a dominion of the British Empire, similar in status to other dominions such as Australia and Canada. While this did grant a measure of self-rule to Ireland, it was more a form of devolution rather than the complete independence many Irish people had hoped for. The treaty also allowed counties in Ireland to opt-out of the agreement if they wished. It was no surprise when the six counties of Ulster decided that they wished to remain in the United Kingdom rather than join the Free State. Ulster therefore became Northern Ireland, a part of the United Kingdom and quite separate from the Irish Free State. For the first time, a border was created between the six counties of Ulster and the rest of Ireland.

Attitudes toward the treaty, which was formally ratified by the Dáil in January 1922, were sharply divided. Many saw it as a pragmatic and logical step toward the final complete independence of Ireland—Michael Collins claimed that the treaty would provide Ireland with "the freedom to achieve freedom." Others disagreed completely, seeing a treaty that left Ulster as part of the United Kingdom and the Irish Free State as nothing more than a British dominion as a betrayal of everything they had been fighting for. In particular, radicals objected to the fact that the treaty required all members of the Irish government to swear an oath of allegiance to Britain. Just hours after signing the treaty, Michael Collins wrote to a friend: "Will anyone be satisfied at the bargain? Will anyone? I tell you this early morning I signed my death warrant."

Many people hoped that the Anglo-Irish Treaty would see an end to the violence that had tormented Ireland for so long. Instead, it would lead to an even more savage war fought between former countrymen.

# Chapter Four

# The Attack on the Four Courts

*"Deputies have spoken about whether dead men would approve of it, and they have spoken whether children yet unborn would approve it, but few have spoken of whether the living approve it."*

—Michael Collins, on the Anglo-Irish Treaty

In the weeks and months following the ratification of the Anglo-Irish Treaty, it became apparent that a split was developing amongst the Irish Republicans. The provisional government supported by moderate members of the IRA sought to support the treaty and to use this as a way of working toward eventual Irish independence. Meanwhile, militants within Sinn Féin and the IRA regarded the treaty as a betrayal and almost immediately began working against it. Some believed that the Free State should undertake an invasion of British-controlled Northern Ireland. Others recognized that they lacked the military capacity to successfully undertake such an attack and claimed that this would lead to the destruction of the Free State.

The disagreement between these two factions, which became known as the Pro-Treaty and Anti-Treaty groups, became bitter and acrimonious. Even the former president, Éamon de Valera, announced that he was against the treaty. Within a relatively short time, argument turned to armed confrontation.

In March 1922, Anti-Treaty members of the IRA held a convention in Dublin at which they formally repudiated the Anglo-Irish Treaty and refused to recognize the authority of the Dáil. One of the leading members of the Anti-Treaty group within the IRA was Rory O'Connor who had lived in Canada before returning in 1915 to join the IRA and take part in the Easter Rising. O'Connor was well-respected within the IRA, and his call for armed opposition to the treaty found many followers. The Anti-Treaty convention met again in early April 1922, and at that meeting, a new constitution for the IRA was adopted. Asked by a journalist whether he wanted to see Ireland ruled by a military dictatorship, O'Connor replied, "You can take it that way if you want."

On April 14, 1922, O'Connor led a force of around 200 armed Anti-Treaty IRA men to occupy the Four Courts, a complex of buildings in the center of Dublin on the banks of the River Liffey comprising the Public Records Office and the Land Registry Office in addition to the courts themselves. This was a deliberate provocation, both to the Pro-Treaty forces and, more significantly, to the British. Several thousand British soldiers were still present in Dublin, awaiting evacuation following the signing of the Anglo-Irish Treaty, and it seems likely that O'Connor hoped to provoke an armed confrontation with these troops.

In the event, the British decided not to respond directly and instead began applying pressure to the Dáil to deal with the occupation. Much of the responsibility for deciding how to respond fell to Michael Collins, who by this time had been appointed president of the provisional government cabinet and was also effectively the commander of the newly formed Irish National Army.

The situation for Collins and the other members of the Dáil was extremely difficult. If they were to maintain their authority, they could not allow what amounted to an armed insurrection in the center of their main city. However, the men occupying the Four Courts were former comrades and men with whom they had a great deal in common. The situation became worse when, on June 22, two members of the IRA assassinated Sir Henry Wilson outside his house in London. Wilson was a prominent Unionist who opposed any form of self-rule for Ireland and owned property in the north. His death sparked outrage in London, and there were suspicions that the assassination had been ordered by Michael Collins.

Tensions increased further on June 26 when a group of Anti-Treaty IRA men who had spent time with their comrades in the Four Courts building left in a convoy of vehicles and headed for a car sales company's premises on Dublin's Lower Baggot Street. While they were attempting to appropriate 16 vehicles, lorries loaded with troops of the Irish National Army arrived. There was a scuffle that resulted in the arrest of all the Anti-Treaty IRA men. English journalist and writer Clare Sheridan watched these events unfold, and she wrote that a man in the crowd turned to her and said: "Something'll sure happen soon; it's working up for a scrap!" Sheridan was also able to interview O'Connor and his men in the Four Courts. When she pointed out that the Anti-Treaty men would not stand a chance if they were attacked either by the National Army or British troops, O'Connor replied grimly, "Then I'll go down in the ruins, or up in the flames."

The British government made it clear that, unless the Irish provisional government was able to remove the occupiers of the Four Courts, Britain would consider using the British troops still present in Ireland to undertake that task and to restore order. The situation became even more grave when the men in the Four Courts kidnapped Jeremiah O'Connell, deputy chief of staff in the Irish National Army. Faced with few alternatives, on June 27, 1922, the provisional government cabinet issued an ultimatum to the men in the Four Courts: evacuate or face immediate military action by the Irish National Army.

By this time, Rory O'Connor had been joined by 12 members of the Executive of the IRA, including Joe McKelvey, the chief of staff, and Liam Mellows, quartermaster general. The 200 men inside were armed with rifles and sub-machine guns as well as two light machine guns and a captured armored car equipped with a Vickers heavy machine gun. Entrances had been barricaded and improvised mines had been planted within the complex. The National Army units facing them had similar weapons but were also equipped with two 18-pounder field-guns provided from the British Army on the orders of the British secretary of state for war, Winston Churchill. This artillery was set up on the opposite side of the River Liffey from the Four Courts complex. It has also been claimed, though never confirmed, that the Irish National

Army was supported by special troops from the British Army.

The ultimatum was delivered to the men inside the Four Courts late in the evening of June 27. Some of those who were inside at the time later said that, as a result, O'Connor and the others decided that they would leave the building at 08:00 the following morning. If that is true, it was too late. At 4 am on June 28, the Irish National Army, using the artillery loaned by the British Army, began a bombardment of the Four Courts. This moment marks the beginning of the Irish Civil War.

## Chapter Five

# Civil War Breaks Out

*"If liberty is not entire it is not liberty."*

—Éamon de Valera

The bombardment of the Four Courts buildings by the field guns used by the Irish National Army proved to be less effective than they had hoped. The guns fired every 15 minutes, but the damage they caused to the Four Courts buildings was not catastrophic and the men inside were able to hold out. Under the orders of Winston Churchill, the British Army provided two additional guns which were quickly added to the battery on the far bank of the Liffey. Churchill also offered to give much heavier 60-pounder howitzers or even to order the RAF to bomb the Four Courts from the air, but both these offers were refused by Michael Collins who was anxious to avoid civilian casualties.

For almost three days, the bombardment continued and both sides took pot-shots at each other. Large crowds of spectators gathered to watch and to photograph the action. Seven men of the National Army were killed by rifle and machine-gun fire and many more were wounded, but still the men inside refused to give up. By the morning of Friday, June 30, parts of the Four Courts complex were in the hands of the National Army but the Anti-Treaty men were still holding out in the small northern block. Fires were raging uncontrolled in some buildings when a huge explosion ripped through the small Records Treasury building on the north-west corner of the complex.

No-one is quite sure what caused this explosion—it may have been caused when fires reached stored explosives or combustible material or when a shell hit explosive material. A huge mushroom cloud of dark smoke rose over the city, and papers from the records office were scattered like confetti over a large part of central Dublin. Despite the explosion, the Anti-Treaty men held out a little longer, hoping that a column of other members of the Anti-Treaty IRA would come to their assistance. When it became clear that this was not likely to happen, the men inside the Four Courts, including Rory O'Connor, surrendered to the National Army. Three had been killed during the fighting and several more were wounded. Jeremiah O'Connell, the kidnapped deputy chief of staff of the National Army, was released unharmed.

Yet the surrender of the men inside the Four Courts did not end what has become known as the Battle of Dublin. Even while the bombardment of the Four Courts was in progress, another group of around 70 Anti-Treaty IRA troops led by their Commandant Cathal Brugha established themselves in a block of buildings on the east side of Sackville Street (now renamed O'Connell Street) in the center of Dublin. This block comprised fourteen buildings including four hotels, and the men inside erected barricades and knocked holes in the walls between the buildings to turn the block into a strongpoint. Senior members of the

Anti-Treaty group including Éamon de Valera joined the men and women inside.

In the early hours of July 3, with the Four Courts in their hands, the National Army turned its attention to Sackville Street. Armored cars raked the block with machine-gun fire while artillery bombarded the buildings. Fierce fighting continued until five o'clock on July 5 when the last building held by Anti-Treaty forces, the Hamman Hotel, was set on fire. Most Anti-Treaty forces still inside surrendered, but Cathal Brugha emerged with his pistol in his hand and was shot by the soldiers waiting outside. He later died of his wounds.

With Dublin now in the hands of the National Army, the remainder of Ireland became split between Pro and Anti-Treaty factions. The Free State controlled only the eastern part of the country. Anti-Treaty forces, also known as "Irregulars," held much of the west of Ireland in addition to the cities of Cork, Limerick, and Waterford in the county of Munster. This latter area became informally known as the "Munster Republic," and it was one of the main strongholds for the Anti-Treaty forces.

The Anti-Treaty IRA had more men than the Free State—under the command of Chief of Staff Liam Lynch, the Anti-Treaty IRA had around 12,000 men, many of them experienced fighters from the War of Independence. In contrast, the National Army had only 8,000 soldiers. Still, the balance of power lay with the National Army under the control of Michael Collins. Both sides had large numbers of rifles and light machine guns but only the National Army had access to regular supplies of ammunition as well as artillery and armored cars borrowed from the British.

Liam Lynch decided on a mainly defensive strategy for the Anti-Treaty forces. He intended to hold out in Munster and other areas, hoping that this would force the Free State to abandon the Anglo-Irish Treaty. On the other side, Michael Collins was determined to end the war as quickly as possible to ensure that the last remaining British troops left Ireland and that control was handed over to the provisional government.

The first city held by Anti-Treaty forces in the Munster Republic to come under attack was Limerick where the National Army began its assault on July 11. As in the fighting on Sackville Street in Dublin, both sides were relatively evenly matched in terms of men, rifles, and machine guns, but only the National Army had field guns and armored cars. Bitter street fighting, which left much of the center of Limerick in ruins, continued until July 21 when the city fell into the hands of the National Army.

By the time that Anti-Treaty resistance in Limerick ended, the National Army had also taken the city of Waterford, again using artillery to overcome the defenders. By August 10, the National Army had also occupied the former Anti-Treaty strongholds of Tipperary, Carrick on Suir, Kilmallock, and Clonmel, giving them almost complete control over the south midlands of Ireland.

While these overland attacks on Anti-Treaty positions were in progress, the National Army also undertook a series of daring seaborne invasions. Several civilian passenger liners were commandeered by the National Army and these, escorted by warships of the British Royal Navy, landed National Army troops at Clew Bay in County Mayo on July 24, and these troops rapidly moved to occupy much of the west of Ireland. The largest attack from the sea took place in the south at Fenit in County Kerry on August 2, where almost 2,000 well-armed and equipped National Army troops were landed. These units quickly occupied the city of Cork and other towns in the area. On August 11, Anti-Treaty forces evacuated the town of Fermoy, the last town of any size which they controlled. In early August, the Anti-Treaty forces had also attempted to use a group of around 200 men to isolate Dublin by destroying all the road and rail bridges that provided access to the city. This was a complete failure, and most of the men involved were quickly captured.

In little more than one month of fighting, the National Army had taken control of virtually every town in the Irish Free State. Partly, this was due to their superiority in artillery to which the Anti-Treaty forces had no effective response. It was also due to a reluctance on the part of many Anti-Treaty IRA groups to fight their former comrades. One member of the Anti-Treaty IRA later said that there was often an unwillingness to fire upon the Free State forces because "the officers who were operating against us were our own former friends."

The members of the National Army seemed much less reluctant to engage in combat or to kill their former colleagues. They were also better disciplined than their foes and better equipped and supplied. These factors help to account for their rapid advance and successes in combat. However, though the National Army now controlled most of the towns and cities in Ireland, that did not mean that they also controlled the rural areas.

Recognizing the inevitable and accepting that the Anti-Treaty IRA could not defeat the National Army in open warfare, on August 11, 1922, Liam Lynch ordered his men to stop attempting to hold fixed positions and instead to fade into the countryside and to pursue a guerilla war against the National Army. The civil war abruptly changed from a conventional series of military engagements into a brutal and bitter clandestine war fought between the remnants of the Anti-Treaty IRA and the National Army of the Irish Free State.

## Chapter Six

# A Bloody Guerilla War

*"The Free State is on the verge of collapse."*

—Liam Lynch

Following the National Army offensives in July and early August, the Anti-Treaty forces were left without control of any large town or city, though they still controlled rural areas in western parts of Cork and Kerry in the south, in County Wexford in the east, and in parts of counties including Sligo and Mayo in the west. The Anti-Treaty forces formed "flying columns," small, mobile groups of fighters who were able to strike within areas nominally controlled by the National Army. This tactic had worked well against the British during the Irish War of Independence.

Most of the actions undertaken by the Anti-Treaty IRA were small-scale, though a few involved larger forces of up to several hundred fighters. In the early hours of August 14, 1922, for example, around 100 men of the Anti-Treaty Fourth Northern Division of the IRA under the command of Frank Aiken attacked the barracks in the town of Dundalk. Ironically, the men defending the town were former members of the Fifth Northern Division of the IRA who were Pro-Treaty and had been inducted into the National Army. Just one month previously, the attackers had themselves occupied these barracks. Two months previously, the two units had been ready to fight together. Now they were pitched against one another.

The Anti-Treaty troops quickly took control of Dundalk, over 300 prisoners were freed, and more than 300 members of the National Army were captured. This was a major although short-lived success for the Anti-Treaty IRA; their troops were unable to hold the town against National Army reinforcements and were quickly driven out.

Other, similar actions took place elsewhere in Ireland. The small town of Kenmare in the south of County Kerry, for example, was taken by Anti-Treaty forces on September 9 and was held against National Army attacks until early December. The town of Clifden in County Galway was attacked by around 350 Anti-Treaty forces on October 29. Other towns, including Bantry in County Cork and Killorglin in County Kerry, were also attacked by Anti-Treaty forces in August and September. Neither was taken but these attacks inflicted large numbers of casualties on the National Army.

Most of the assaults undertaken by the Anti-Treaty forces during this period were on a smaller scale. They attacked National Army patrols and personnel in Dublin throughout August and September. A National Army soldier was assassinated while visiting his family in County Tipperary on August 19. On August 20, a party of National Army soldiers traveling in a car in County Cork was ambushed. One was killed, two wounded, and the remainder taken prisoner. On August 26, a National Army column of 100 troops was ambushed in County Kerry. On September 2, Anti-Treaty men driving a captured armored car attacked the city of Macroom in County Cork but withdrew after a firefight with National Army troops which lasted for more than seven hours. On the same day, a group of National Army troops were undergoing drill instruction in the city of Cork when a truck driven by Anti-Treaty IRA drew up and opened fire with a machine gun, killing two and wounding six.

These are examples only—barely a day in August and September of 1922 passed without an attack on members of the National Army, an assassination, or an attempt to disrupt infrastructure such as the blowing up of a railway bridge on the Cork-Dublin line. The guerilla war was effective in inflicting casualties on the forces of the Free State, but it did little to change the course of the war. However, other events in August were to throw the Irish Free State into crisis and precipitate a new and even more brutal phase of the civil war.

## Chapter Seven

# The Deaths of Arthur Griffith and Michael Collins

*"Yerra, they'll never shoot me in my own county."*

—Michael Collins

During August of 1922, the Irish Free State was rocked by the deaths of two of its most prominent members. Arthur Griffith was one of the men who had undertaken treaty negotiations with Britain, and by this point, he was serving as the president of the second Dáil Éireann, having taken over from Éamon de Valera after a vote in January.

During the first week of August, 51-year-old Arthur Griffith had been confined to the hospital following a serious case of tonsillitis, but against the advice of medical staff, he returned to work almost straight after. On the morning of Saturday, August 12, at around ten o'clock, he was preparing to leave his home to go to his office when he stopped and bent forward to re-tie his shoelace. Griffith collapsed to the floor, unconscious. He quickly came to and was helped to his feet but collapsed again, blood flowing freely from his mouth. Doctors were called, but they were unable to save Griffith who died a short time later. The cause of death was a cerebral hemorrhage (though it was mistakenly reported at the time as a heart attack), and Griffith was buried four days later.

Arthur Griffith was seen as a moderate by many in the Free State and his loss was a serious blow, even though his role as president had become that of a mere figurehead by the time his death. This blow was quickly followed by another even more serious loss to the Free State less than two weeks later.

By August of 1922, Michael Collins was the most powerful man in the Free State government. He was commander-in-chief of the National Army and personally responsible for the direction of Free State forces. In public, Collins was a strong supporter of the Free State and in favor of the war to suppress Anti-Treaty forces. In private, however, he was extremely ambivalent about the war itself. Many of the troops he was directing the National Army against were IRA men with whom he had fought in the War of Independence. He felt pressured to fight them by the threats of the British government to intervene if the Free State was not able to maintain effective control over Ireland. It seems that what he wanted more than anything was an end to the war.

Although he was feeling ill and feverish, Michael Collins left Dublin in a convoy of National Army troops on August 20. The formal purpose of his trip was to inspect National Army units, but he also planned to visit prisons where members of the Anti-Treaty forces were being held and to meet with neutral members of the IRA to discuss how the civil war could be brought to an end. Collins was accompanied by his friend and the major general of the National Army, Emmet Dalton.

By the evening of August 22, the convoy which comprised a motorcycle, a small truck carrying several National Army troops, an armored car, and an open car in which Collins and Dalton were passengers, was traveling through south Cork, through the valley called Béal na mBláth, around ten miles from the town of Bandon. Suddenly, in the failing light of sunset, shots rang out as the vehicles were ambushed by a force of around 30 Anti-Treaty men.

Dalton told the driver to try to escape. Collins immediately countermanded this by telling him, "Stop, we'll fight them." When the vehicles stopped, Collins ran forward and began shooting at the ambushers. Moments later, he was struck in the head by a bullet and died soon after. Collins was the only person killed on either side in the ambush.

The death of Michael Collins was a staggering blow to the Free State. A London newspaper noted that "the death of Collins leaves the ship of the Free State without a helmsman." There was immense anger amongst the National Army men, and a desire to take revenge against those who had killed their commander-in-chief. On the day after Collins' death, Richard Mulcahy, National Army chief of staff, issued a statement to the whole army which noted: "Stand calmly by your posts. Bend bravely and undaunted to your task. Let no cruel act of reprisal blemish your bright honor."

Still, the death of Michael Collins quickly led to the next phase of the Irish Civil War, where reprisals and atrocities were not just permitted but officially sanctioned.

## Chapter Eight
# Executions and Assassinations

*"Take a step or two forward, lads, it will be easier that way."*

—The last words of Erskine Childers before his execution by firing squad.

Following the death of Michael Collins and in the face of escalating guerilla warfare on the part of the Anti-Treaty IRA, the Free State provisional government, under the new leadership of William Thomas Cosgrave, Richard Mulcahy, and Kevin O'Higgins, took a different approach. They decided that the Anti-Treaty IRA were criminals rather than combatants and were therefore not owed the courtesies due to prisoners of war. On September 27, 1922, the Dáil approved the Army Emergency Powers Resolution which allowed military tribunals to impose severe penalties for a whole range of offenses. Possession of any firearm or even a single cartridge could be punished by death by firing squad. This meant that any captured member of the Anti-Treaty IRA carrying a weapon or ammunition could be legally executed. This was strengthened in early 1923 to permit the execution of Anti-Treaty sympathizers who had done nothing more than carrying messages.

On October 10, 1922, the Catholic Church in Ireland issued a statement noting that anyone taking part in Anti-Treaty activities was "guilty of grievous sins and may not be absolved in Confession nor admitted to the Holy Communion if they persist in such evil courses." In effect, every member of the Anti-Treaty movement was being excommunicated from the Catholic Church. With more than 90% of its members being Catholic, this was a severe blow to the Anti-Treaty movement.

The execution of Anti-Treaty prisoners began almost immediately. Seven prisoners were executed in Dublin in November. On November 17, the author Erskine Childers, the man who had supplied arms to the IRA during the War of Independence, was arrested in Dublin. He was found to be carrying a small, Spanish pocket pistol (which had originally been given to him by Michael Collins). Childers was summarily executed on November 24.

Many executions of prisoners were carried out not as a punishment for crimes but as reprisals for killings by Anti-Treaty members. A National Army order issued in February 1923 noted that "in every case of outrage in any battalion area, three men will be executed. No clemency will be shown in any case." On December 7, Anti-Treaty men shot and killed Sean Hales, a member of the Dáil. In reprisal for this attack, four Anti-Treaty prisoners being held in prison in Dublin were executed. One of those was Rory O'Connor, the man who had led the occupation of the Four Courts which precipitated the civil war. One of the members of the cabinet who approved these executions, Kevin O'Higgins, had been the Best Man at O'Connor's wedding just a few months before.

Executions continued throughout the remainder of 1922 and into 1923. Some of these reprisal killings were bestial in their savagery. One of the most notorious occurred in County Kerry on March 7, 1923. In response to the killing of five National Army soldiers by a booby-trap bomb, nine Anti-Treaty prisoners were tied in a circle at a crossroads in a forest in Ballyseedy. A large landmine was placed in the center of the circle and detonated from a distance. One man, Stephen Fuller, survived and managed to escape. For days afterward, crows flocked to the area, eating the flesh, entrails, and body-parts blasted into the trees.

In total, 81 prisoners were officially executed by the Free State, more than twice as many as were executed by the British during the whole of the War of Independence. Not all the killings were judicial executions, and the number of unofficial executions was significantly higher. In 1921, Michael Collins had ordered the formation of the Criminal Investigation Department (CID), an armed, plainclothes section of the national police force. A number of killings of Anti-Treaty supporters were attributed to the CID during the period of the civil war including the murder of five people on August 26 and 29, 1922, whose bodies were found dumped in the suburbs of Dublin. In total, it is believed than anything up to 150 people were summarily executed by Free State forces without any legal process.

These killings left a legacy of bitterness which was to pervade Ireland for decades to come, and they did not end with the civil war. Noel Lemass, a man who had been a captain in the Anti-Treaty IRA, was abducted by National Army troops in Dublin in July 1923—two months after the civil war ended. His body was found in the Dublin

Mountains, near Glencree, in October of 1923. Kevin O'Higgins, Rory O'Connor's former friend who had voted for his execution, was assassinated by members of the IRA in 1927.

Nevertheless, there were those who claimed that these executions helped the Irish Free State to combat the Anti-Treaty IRA in the only way possible. The National Army was far more powerful in the field than the Anti-Treaty IRA, but it was difficult to combat assassinations and guerilla attacks by using conventional military tactics.

The Anti-Treaty forces reacted initially to the wave of executions with even more violence targeted at the National Army and the Free State authorities. Liam Lynch, leader of the Anti-Treaty IRA, issued what became known as the "orders of frightfulness" in November 1922. These allowed the assassination of members of the Dáil as well as judges and newspaper editors who were seen as friendly to the Pro-Treaty cause. These killings included the assassination of Kevin O'Higgins' father in February 1923 and the burning of a number of large houses in the Irish countryside which were owned by people who supported the Free State.

# Chapter Nine

# The End of the Civil War

*"If five men are arrested in each area, we are finished."*

—Tom Crofts, leader of the Cork Brigades of the Anti-Treaty IRA

By the beginning of 1923, support for the Anti-Treaty forces in Ireland was waning. The condemnation by the Catholic Church was a factor, as was the knowledge that any act of violence against the Free State or the National Army was likely to lead to reprisal executions. There was also a general weariness amongst the population for continuing violence and a general desire to return to a more settled and normal life.

Thirty-two Anti-Treaty supporters were executed in January 1923, and in February, W. T. Cosgrave, who had become chairman of the provisional government on the death of Michael Collins, noted that "the executions have had a remarkable effect. It is a sad thing to say, but it is nevertheless the case." Chillingly, Cosgrave went on to add that "if the country is to live and if we have to exterminate 10,000 republicans, the 3 millions of our people are bigger than the 10,000." It was clear that the resolve of those running the Free State and their determination to suppress the Anti-Treaty IRA without British intervention were as strong as ever.

On the Anti-Treaty side, many people were beginning to wonder whether it was possible to win this war at all or whether the cost was worth it. Dan Breen, the leader of an Anti-Treaty IRA flying column in Tipperary, told other senior members of the group that "in order to win this war you'll need to kill three out of every five people in the country and it isn't worth it."

Despite a falling-off of support, during February 1923, attacks by Anti-Treaty IRA flying columns continued. On February 3, an Anti-Treaty unit attacked the railway station at Killala in County Mayo, destroying the station buildings and setting a train on fire before sending it off down the track to crash. On February 4, National Army troops in Bandon in County Cork used Anti-Treaty prisoners to clear a road that was suspected of being mined. They drove the prisoners down the road and two were killed when a hidden mine exploded. On February 7, another Anti-Treaty IRA group attacked a National Army post in Ballinamore in County Leitrim. The post was destroyed and more than 30 prisoners taken.

Despite these continuing attacks, the Free State announced on February 8, a suspension of all executions until February 18 and an amnesty for any Anti-Treaty IRA fighters who surrendered before that date. On February 10, a senior officer in the Anti-Treaty forces, Tom Barry, suggested that the IRA call a truce but this was quickly rejected by Liam Lynch, the commander of the Anti-Treaty IRA. On February 26, a meeting of senior officers of the Anti-Treaty IRA was convened at Ballinageary in County Tipperary. Many units reported grave shortages of men and supplies—officers of the First Southern Division told the leadership that "in a short time we would not have a man left owing to the great number of arrests and casualties." Other units reported a similar situation, but Liam Lynch refused to countenance any form of truce or cease-fire.

During March 1923, the attacks, assassinations, and executions continued. Most were on a small scale with the exception of an extended gun battle between National Army forces and around 100 Anti-Treaty IRA men in the town of Charlestown in County Mayo. On March 24, the Executive of the Anti-Treaty IRA met again, this time in County Tipperary. Once again, Tom Barry suggested that the war must be ended. Once again, this suggestion was rejected, and Liam Lynch re-stated his determination to continue.

In early April, acting on information received from Anti-Treaty prisoners, Free State forces began conducting large-scale operations in the Knockmealdown Mountains in south Tipperary and Waterford. Within a short time, they arrested a number of leaders of the Anti-Treaty IRA including Dan Breen and Todd Andrews and large numbers of IRA fighters. A few days later, a group of Anti-Treaty IRA was caught in the open on a hillside in the mountains. When they attempt to flee, Free State forces open fire. Some Anti-Treaty men were killed and the others were captured. One of the dead was discovered to be Liam Lynch.

On April 11, the leader of the IRA flying column in Waterford, Tom Keating, was killed during a firefight. On April 14, Austin Stack, the deputy IRA chief of staff was captured near Ballymacarbry. A statement issued by the National Army at this time noted that "events of the past few days point to the beginning of the end as a far as the irregular campaign is concerned."

On April 22, Free State troops surrounded a house in Castlebellingham in the Dundalk area. Inside were Frank Aiken, the new head of the Anti-Treaty IRA and his two most senior leaders, brothers Padraig and Sean Quinn. In the firefight that followed, Sean Quinn was killed and Padraig Quinn captured, but Frank Aiken somehow managed to escape.

Accepting the inevitable, on April 30, Aiken ordered all Anti-Treaty IRA units to stop fighting. Most did, but some sporadic violence continued. A National Army sergeant was shot dead while on sentry duty on May 6, and on May 15, the last armed confrontation of the Irish Civil War took place at Valleymount in County Wicklow when Free State forces attacked an Anti-Treaty IRA flying column led by Ned Plunkett. Plunkett was killed in the subsequent gun-battle and the other members of the column were captured.

On May 24, 1923, Frank Aiken ordered all Anti-Treaty IRA units to "dump" their arms—in other words, to hide them for potential future use. There was no formal surrender by Anti-Treaty forces, no peace treaty, and no handover of weapons, but this moment marks the effective end of the Irish Civil War. On the same day, Éamon de Valera issued an emotional and emotive statement: "Soldiers of the Republic. Legion of the Rearguard: The Republic can no longer be defended successfully by your arms. Further sacrifice of life would now be in vain and the continuance of the struggle in arms unwise in the national interest and prejudicial to the future of our cause. Military victory must be allowed to rest for the moment with those who have destroyed the Republic."

# Chapter Ten

# Aftermath

*"Civil war is not about conquest or economics, but about how a nation will govern itself. There are no winners."*

—Eoin Neeson

No-one is certain how many people died during the Irish Civil War. Estimates range from 1,500 to 4,000. After the announcement of the cease-fire in April 1923, around 12,000 Anti-Treaty prisoners were still being held by the Free State. Most were not released until 1924 following a protracted hunger strike in which several prisoners died.

Even after the war, the legacy of bitterness led to sporadic violence. When the bodies of three Anti-Treaty IRA men executed in January 1923 were buried in Dundalk in November 1924, a gunfight erupted between armed Anti-Treaty men and Free State troops leaving one man dead and several wounded. The IRA only officially renounced attacks on the Free State in 1948, at the time of the creation of the Republic of Ireland. After that time, the IRA directed its efforts toward attacks on the British and the creation of a united Ireland.

In Ireland, the civil war caused bitterness and hatred which was to last for decades. Pro-Treaty followers felt that the Anti-Treaty IRA were in danger of halting progress toward the only solution which would finally bring independence to Ireland. Anti-Treaty followers saw the Irish Free State as a British-sponsored instrument of repression and regarded their agreement to the establishment of Northern Ireland as a betrayal.

Michael Collins and his Pro-Treaty followers were right—the creation of the Irish Free State did eventually lead to complete independence for most of Ireland. In 1926, Éamon de Valera and Frank Aiken decided to enter constitutional politics and formed the Fianna Fáil party which would eventually go on to be an important factor in the political scene in Ireland. In 1927, members of Fianna Fáil took the oath of allegiance to Britain and entered the Dáil. By doing this, they recognized the legitimacy of the Irish Free State. Pro-Treaty followers coalesced into the Fine Gael party.

In elections in 1932, Fianna Fáil took control of the Dáil under the leadership of Éamon de Valera. In 1937, they were able to pass a new constitution that did not include an oath of allegiance to Britain and made the president the head of state of Ireland. This independence was sufficient to allow the Irish Free State to declare itself neutral during World War II. In 1948, a collation government which included both Fianna Fáil and Fine Gael left the British Commonwealth completely and created the independent Republic of Ireland.

The issue of the six counties of Ulster which became Northern Ireland remained a problem for both Ireland and Britain. Many people in the Republic of Ireland believed that Ulster should be part of a united Ireland and not part of the United Kingdom. The Protestant majority in Northern Ireland refused to accept this, and the violence which began in Northern Ireland and Britain in the late 1960s and continued to the late 1990s was directly related to this issue. Although Northern Ireland has been generally peaceful since the signing of the Good Friday Agreement in 1998, the relationship between Northern Ireland and the Republic of Ireland continues to be a problem. Even during the negotiations toward Britain's exit from the European Union (Brexit), the question of how to deal with the border between Northern Ireland and the Republic of Ireland has become one of the most significant and most intractable problems.

# Conclusion

The Irish Civil War came close to tearing apart the newly created Irish Free State. Instead of unifying Ireland, the Anglo-Irish Treaty created divisions between Northern Ireland and the Free State and between pro and anti factions within the Free State. The issue was the same one which would dog Irish politics for the next one hundred years—how to reconcile the desire of many people in the south and west for independence with the wishes of people in the north to remain a part of the United Kingdom. The outcome was a compromise which created as many problems as it solved.

When faced with armed opposition to the treaty, the people who governed the Free State were presented with an impossible situation—if they declared war on their former comrades, they risked dividing the new state. If they did not, they risked the direct intervention of Britain and the loss of the measure of independence they had gained.

While Michael Collins remained an important figure in the Free State, the general approach seems to have been motivated by a desire to end the civil war as quickly as possible and with as little bloodshed as possible. With his death, the war fought by the Free State changed to include the execution of prisoners, extra-judicial killing, and even assassination and murder. It is possible that these brutal methods helped to win the war, but they left a legacy of bitterness and hatred that would pervade Ireland for decades to come.

The Irish Civil War was short, and the total number of casualties was relatively low, but an understanding of the origins and outcome of this conflict is essential to an understanding of the progress of Ireland toward independence.

Printed in Great Britain
by Amazon